Gusto

BY KATE & MARCO ANZANI

*A restaurateurs journey over 15 years to celebrate
love of ingredients, celebrations and sustainability*

LitPrime Solutions
21250 Hawthorne Blvd
Suite 500, Torrance, CA 90503
www.litprime.com
Phone: 1-800-981-9893

Published by LitPrime Solutions: 10/27/2023

ISBN: 979-8-88703-056-2(sc)
ISBN: 979-8-88703-057-9(e)

Library of Congress Control Number: 2022918138

LitPrime
"Your story is our priority"

To our three children:
Azzurra, Ambra
and Alessia
Live Life intently
in Gusto.

This is dedicated to
my Grandmother
"Ching"
Who's memory in
our Heart Lives

Table of Contents

A Heart of Gratitude. 6

This is Anzani. 7

Our Story 9

Authors' Biography 10

Anzani's Cuisine

APPETIZERS

TOMATO
BREAD
16

TOMATO
SOFRITO / SOUP
16

TOMATO
CHIPS
17

ROASTED RED PEPPER SOUP AND ROASTED TOMATO
SOUP WITH BATTER FRED ASPARAGUS
21

OVEN DRIED TOMATOES
FOR SALADS
23

ZOLA (GORGONZOLA)
PANNACOTTA WITH
MUSCAT GRAPE
25

SALMON
GRAVLAX
26

CHICKPEA
FALAFEL
34

A VERY GREEN
FALAFEL RECIPE
36

A FLUFFY
HUMMUS RECIPE
37

BEETROOT
HUMMUS RECIPE
38

MEDITERRANEAN
BEETROOT HUMMUS
38

FLATBREAD
DOUGH
39

FLATBREAD WITH ROASTED
GARLIC, SUN-DRIED TOMATO
AND BUFALA CHEESES
42

ANZANI
CHEESE FUNDUE
44

TUSCAN
BEAN SOUP
46

MAIN COURSES

PORK TOMAHAWK WITH
CHIKEN MUSHROOM
50

ANGUS TENDERLOIN
WITH CAULIFLOWER
STEAK AND HARISSA
52

PORK BELLY ROAST
WITH PURPLE YAM AND
BANANA BLOSSOM
54

STEAK ON GRILL WITH
HERB BUTTER AND ROSEMARY
56

CHICKEN TANGINE WITH
PRESERVED LEMONS
58

LAMB TANGINE
WITH PRUNES
60

BEEF KABOB
MORROCAN SPICES
62

PUMPKIN FLOWERS STUFFED
WITH RICOTTA CHEESE
64

LOBSTER RISOTTO WITH
66

SMOKED
RIBS
68

CRISPY ROLL OF PORK WITH
FIGS, PRUNES AND ALMONDS
STUFFED WITH HERBED
LEMON BREAD STUFFING
70

BLACK COD WRAPPED
IN POTATO SPAGHETTI
WITH LEMON AND WHITE
WINE REDUCTION
72

CAULIFLOWER VELOUTE
AND KALE BED WITH
AND EDIBLE FLOWERS
74

PASTAS

BEETROOT
CARAMELE PASTA
78

RAVIOLI
80

BASIC PASTA
DOUGH RECIPE
82

EGG PASTA
DOUGH
84

LINGUINI
VOGOLE
86

SQUID INK
SPAGHETTI
88

OPEN SPINACH LASAGNA
WITH FOIE GRAS AND TRUFFLE CREAM
90

Closing 91

A Heart of Gratitude

If you don't train your mind to appreciate what is good, you'll look for something better for the future, even when things are great.

True Story: Appreciate What you have. Not Everyone has it. Look around your own backyard.

What to expect ?

This cookbook seeded during the end of 2019. Got stuck in recipe development 2020 (lockdown included) By 2021 what we set out to do did not match the cooking or kind of people we once were. After taking part of a city food bank, Founding of a city Wide food and Wine Festival and developing a City Farmers market during the hardest of lockdown, We recognized the Menu & ingredients (or lack of) was giving us real clues How the future looks like. There were real cravings to remind US of our childhood memories for comfort, there was a need to recreate dishes to feel secure & safe. Food plays such an important role in our survival as a human race to happiness. We also needed to incorporate high nutrition, protein packed recipes and high energy meals without losing the flavour. The market was not open for high presentation, complicated meals. They wanted high flavour, accessible ingredients. We also realized everyone started to cook. We got phone calls on How to reduce stock properly & If they can freeze them. Questions on How to make it dynamic in flavour. (high concentration stock, finish with cooking Marsala Wine) phone calls from the US came on How to recreate my grandmothers tamales, Biko and Lumpia. Love for bananas & Coconut.

This book is the RoadMap of Cross - Cultural Food. Marco is Italian (but lived in 45 countries) married to me with Asian Roots (Chinese-Filipino- Spanish heritage) Our life Isnt Third culture. But it once was. We have lived in China, Malaysia, Indonesia, UAE, Most of North America & Europe. Many can relate to Cross Cultural marriages, expect collaborative recipes and unique pictures of heritage ingredients while incorporating recipes for everyday, batch cooking and some entertaining menus. So did exactly that. Gusto, Second Edition 2023 Release.

This is Anzani

Pre pandemic, we were using 80 percent imported Ingredients. By 2022 we were using 30 percent imported, 70 percent locally sourced. We were awarded by Green Choice Philippines as 1 out of 3 sustainable restaurants in the Philippines, measured against ISO practices. We feel good to be ahead of the pack. But also, we wanted to share this practice as it is important to be able to move forward sustainably (this means everlasting, consistent and never losing cadence or standard)

It is also very important for US to honour the long standing Food currency of the Italian country. My husband is very Italian, and in So many ways, I have crossed over to the Italian way of Life. More So eating habits, excellence of produce and purist in technique. There is So much respect for food provenance and Regional cooking.

Our cookbook Will share a pizza recipe base, breads, tomato Sofrito, Smoked soups. Ask for a Pork tomahawk (from your Local butcher). You Will learn How to use Salmon 6 different ways using dehydration, curing, smoking, grilling Pan fry & soft poaching.

Our Story

Supporting Farms & Communties

Our restaurants were very reliant on accredited suppliers and distributors. Our relationships were the Middle men pre pandemic.

After a hard lockdown, the need from farm to Plate needed to become more consistent. As grocery stores had become incredibly pricey and as distributors and suppliers couldnt restock as fast as they wanted to. We practice one tier sourcing more often post pandemic or grow our own.

We work with the farms locally to grow specific Vegetables, creating a sustainable cycle of supplier chain management. The volume of our restaurants would Command 100 kilos of Meat a week, 30 kilos of Vegetables at a time. There was a need for a vertical farm supply system. Then one day we called them in and the farm coops, and asked them All to display weekly in a parking lot to Help Their needs of distribution and our need for produce. The Saturday Farmers Market was born.

Why do we do What we do. Why we do it

Chefs during lockdown All started accepting jobs in cruise ships. Hotel chefs started moving to different industries. We were reeling, trying to hold them off. Pleading to stay in the industry. Thank God for government alliance and recovery projects, that we soon created the Food and Wine Festival. Which we hope and work hard to sustain.

The Farmers are in need to be equipped with tools and guidance by businesses. We have been holding hands and supporting community farms to grow specific sizes with guaranteed sales.

The integrated system food supply chain management and the chefs (special skills) were All going to cruise ships. We said " waaaait, we need your talent here " dont leave.

In a nutshell, the industry is changing. But the recipes Will stay. This one is worth passing on.

CHEF MARCO ANZANI is from Como, Italy. He founded many global restaurant concepts on over 5 continents, signature brands in 45 countries, and Michelin-stamped restaurants in 100 cities in the world.

Hailed as the Founder of New Mediterranean Cuisine by the New York Times and a Masterchef.

KATE DYCHANGCO-ANZANI

Multi-Hyphenate.

Author, Entrepreneur, Change-Maker.

With a Bachelor's Degree in Restaurant and Hotel Management from Ambassador to Le Cordon Bleu Philippines and a Masters in Food and Wine gastronomy Harvard Innovation Lab, she is the President of Anzani MK Venture Holding Inc.

Kate is the Co-Founder of Philippine Food and Wine Festivals (Luzon. Visayas. Mindanao) and the Saturday Farmers Market. She is the Author of Gusto

Their Brands in Hospitality is Awarded By Green Choice Philippines (Anzani) Alliance with the WWF on ISO Sustainable Practices, Speaker for TedX, Host to MyTV Channel AnyoneCanCook and Food & Entertaining Editor to Eatz Magazine.

Actively part of the business community and on the Food Tourism Board.

She champions Local ingredients reimagined in 100 ways. Her strong belief is that If you want to know about a culture you look at the country's food.

Tomato Bread

8 slices ripe tomato

1 tbsp. olive oil

2 medium-size red onions, thinly sliced

1 tbsp. balsamic vinegar

2 teaspoons chopped fresh thyme

4 Kilo loaf enriched frozen white bread dough, thawed

50 grams freshly grated Parmesan cheese

¼ teaspoon dried crushed red pepper, minced

1. Arrange tomato slices on rack. Sprinkle with salt. Let stand 30 minutes.
2. Meanwhile, heat oil in heavy large skillet over medium-high heat. Add onions and sauté until very soft, about 15 minutes. Add vinegar and thyme. Sauté until liquid is absorbed, about 2 minutes. Remove from heat.
3. Preheat oven to 195°C. Line 2 baking sheets with parchment paper. Place bread dough on lightly floured work surface Knead cheese and red pepper into dough. Divide dough into 8 equal pieces. Form each piece into ball. Roll out each ball to 3 ½-inch round. Arrange on prepared baking sheets, spacing evenly. Using spoon, make depression in center of each round. Spoon onion mixture into each depression. Top each with 1 tomato slice; press gently to secure. Bake until breads are golden about 30 minutes. Transfer to rack and cool completely. Serve in Anzani Little Clay Pots.

Tomato Sofrito / Soup

The easiest recipe with a technique that no chefs tell you. The trick is to separate the skin.

1 kilo San Marzano Tomatoes

1 garlic head

2 onion

1-liter vegetable water

¼ cup olive oil

Salt to taste

1. Boil water, and soak the tomatoes. Have ice water on standby. Let the tomatoes sit in a cold bath. Peel the tomato skins.
2. In a saucepan, sauté garlic, onion, and olive oil. Set aside. Put the peeled tomatoes in an oven. Caramelize and concentrate the flavors for at least 20 minutes. 180 degrees.
3. In another tray, dehydrate the tomato skins at a lower temperature. To dry and create tomato chips
4. In the same saucepan of sautéed garlic, place the roasted tomatoes in the

pan, with olive oil. Add 1 liter of vegetable stock. Simmer for 10 minutes. Add salt and pepper.

5. Blend. You will reach a deep red tomato sofrito base. Thick and textured. Serve with tomato chips.
6. We usually serve at room temperature with a spoon of basil sorbet. To add more dynamic flavor

A winning dish!

Tomato Chips

~~~~~~

15 tomatoes blackened /charred
3 Tables pond chopped shallot
½ tao dried thyme
1 tbsp butter
3 large bell peppers charred / and peeled
200 Mililiters chicken broth
30 mililiiters cream
Fresh lemon juice to taste
Salt

1. Using the tomato skins. Place Face down in 80 degree oven, sprinkle with salt and thyme (dried or fresh). If you can find fresh thyme.
2. Slow heat dehydrates and crisps the skin. Taking out the moisture. Crispy tomato skins are the result
3. If using a dehydrator: Turn dehydrator setting to 60-80 degrees. Leave the skins in the dehydrator and cover in jar. Youll have Crispy tomato skins to much for snacks or to Add to finish a dish.

Roasted Red Pepper and Roasted Tomato Soup with Battered Asparagus

INGREDIENTS FOR THE PEPPER SOUP:

3 tablespoons fi nely chopped shallot

½ teaspoon dried thyme

1 tablespoon butter

6 red bell peppers, roasted and chopped coarse

200 milliliters chicken broth plus additional to thin the soup

30 milliliters cream

Fresh lemon juice to taste

INGREDIENTS FOR THE TOMATO SOUP:

1 kilo plum tomatoes, quartered lengthwise

3 unpeeled large garlic cloves

3 tablespoons fi nely chopped shallot

½ teaspoon dried oregano

1 tablespoon butter

200 milliliters chicken broth plus additional to thin the soup

30 milliliters cream

Fresh lemon juice to taste

Preparations make batter and fry asparagus

1. Whisk together flour, salt, zest, and pepper in a bowl until combined, then add beer, whisking until smooth.
2. Heat the oil in a heavy saucepan over moderately high heat until it registers 180°C. Submerge asparagus spears in batter to coat half. Working in batches, drag 1 at a time gently against rim to remove excess batter, and then transfer to oil and fry, stirring gently to keep asparagus from sticking together, until golden, 2 to 3 minutes.

Make the pepper soup

1. Using a long-handled fork char the peppers over an open flame, turning them, for 2 to 3 minutes, or until the skins are blackened.
2. Transfer the peppers to a bowl and let them steam, covered, until they are cool enough to handle. Keeping the peppers whole, peel them starting at the blossom end, cut off the tops, and discard the seeds and ribs.
3. In a heavy saucepan cook the shallot, the thyme, and salt and pepper to taste in the butter over moderately low heat, stirring, until the shallot is soft, add the bell peppers and the broth, and simmer the mixture, covered, for 12 to 15 minutes, or until the peppers are very soft. In a blender purée the soup in batches until it is very smooth, forcing it as it is puréed through a fine sieve set over the pan, cleaned, and whisk in the cream, enough of the additional broth to reach the desired consistency, the lemon juice, and salt and pepper to taste.

INGREDIENTS FOR ASPARAGUS:

1 cup all-purpose fl our
1 teaspoon salt
1 tablespoon fi nely grated fresh
    lemon zest
¼ teaspoon black pepper
150 milliliter of pilsner Beer
1 liter vegetable oil
250 grams medium green
    asparagus

Make the tomato soup

1. Spread the tomatoes, skin side down, in one layer in 2 foillined jelly-roll pans, add the garlic to 1 of the pans, and bake the tomatoes and the garlic in a preheated 190°C. Oven for 45 minutes to 1 hour, or until the tomatoes are very soft and their skin is dark brown. Let the tomatoes and the garlic cool in the pans on racks. In a heavy saucepan cook the shallot, the oregano, salt and pepper to taste in the butter over moderately low heat, stirring, until the shallot is soft, add the tomatoes, the garlic and the broth, and simmer the mixture, covered, for 15 minutes. In a blender purée the soup in batches until it is very smooth, forcing it as it is puréed through a fine sieve set over the pan, cleaned, and whisk in the cream, the additional broth if necessary, the lemon juice, and salt and pepper to taste.

2. Mix the two Soups and serve in warm deep plate with one grilled thick slice of Ciabatta Bread,

Oven Dried Tomatoes for Salads

Kept in Preserving Jar. We constantly have these munchies in our fridge. They are So easy to make in the oven, and can be customized to be as herby, garlicky, spicy or seasoned with vinegar as you prefer. They can be made with all types of tomatoes, either small batch or large batch. Homemade sun-dried tomatoes are also usually cheaper than those pricey jars being sold. They are just so incredibly flavorful, especially made with ripe or sour tomatoes. You can alter the flavour to tangy or Sweet

20 cherry or mid Size tomatoes.
fine sea salt

1. Prep your tomatoes. Super simple — just slice the tomatoes in half lengthwise*, spread them out in an even layer cut-side-up on a parchment-covered baking sheet, then season with salt.
2. Slow roast. Now comes the patient part — the tomatoes will need to slow-roast in the oven for about 2.5 to 3.5 hours at low heat (250°F), or until they reach your desired level of dryness.
3. Serve or store. Then once your tomatoes are done, they're ready to serve or add to a recipe right away!

If you want the tomatoes to reduce with slight tang. Add vinegar /oil/thyme. Or If you want slightly sweeter Add 1 tsp to mixture

1. Heat oven to 250°F. Line a large baking sheet with parchment paper.
2. Slice the tomatoes in half lengthwise. Place them cut-side-up on the baking sheet.
3. Bake for 2.5 to 3.5 hours, or until the tomatoes are dried out, keeping an eye on the tomatoes so that they don't burn.
4. Remove from the oven. Serve immediately. Or to store, transfer the sun-dried tomatoes to a jar and fill with olive oil until the tomatoes are completely covered. Add in any desired seasonings (such as a clove of garlic and/or herbs/ vinegar-oil), then cover and refrigerate for up to 4 days.

Zola (Gorgonzola) Pannacotta with Muscat Grape

1 packet gelatin or Agar
   powder
250ml pouring cream
200 thickened cream
250 grams creamy gorgonzola

FOR MUSCAT OR GRAPE REDUCTION:
½ cup Muscat wine or white wine
½ cup sugar
Handful of Grapes
2tbsp gelatin powder

1. Place the creams in a saucepan, sprinkle with gelatin and combine with a whisk.
2. Let stand for 5 minutes to allow agar to steep
3. Warm on medium heat until boiling point is reached then simmer the mixture for 2-3 minutes while stirring, until the consistency changes slightly. All gelatin sediment must dissolve
4. Remove from heat and whisk in the cheese. Stir until well combined.
5. Pour into prepared round moulds, or one big mould. cover and chill for 20 minutes

MUSCAT OR GRAPE REDUCTION:
1. Cook grapes with sugar (¼)
2. Boil white wine with remaining sugar add gelatin sheet or powder. Pour over set Pannacotta.
3. Refrigerate. Then serve

Salmon Gravlax

2 tbsp grated lemon rind
2 tbsp Orange rind
8 juniper berries (crushed and powdered)
2 cup(s) salt
1 cup(s) sugar
1 Tsp allspice

1. Combine all salt, sugar and spices. Mix them well to form dry rub. Set aside while prepping salmon.
2. Place salmon on wire rack inside a sheet pan generously sprinkle the salmon with dry rub, really be liberal with it to coat entire flesh. Cover salmon with plastic wrap and refrigerate for at least 10 hours or overnight.
3. Rinse Salmon & take out excess marinade. Place salmon back on rack on sheet pan and put back in refrigerator uncovered for at least 2 hours. This will help smoke to stick to salmon when smoking it.
4. To smoke salmon: place in large plastic container with lid. Using smoke gun or any cold smoking device, pump smoke into container until it is full then add lid. When smoke has fully dissipated, repeat smoking process up to two more times to ensure enough smoke flavor.
5. Slice salmon into thin slices and serve with favorite brunch items.

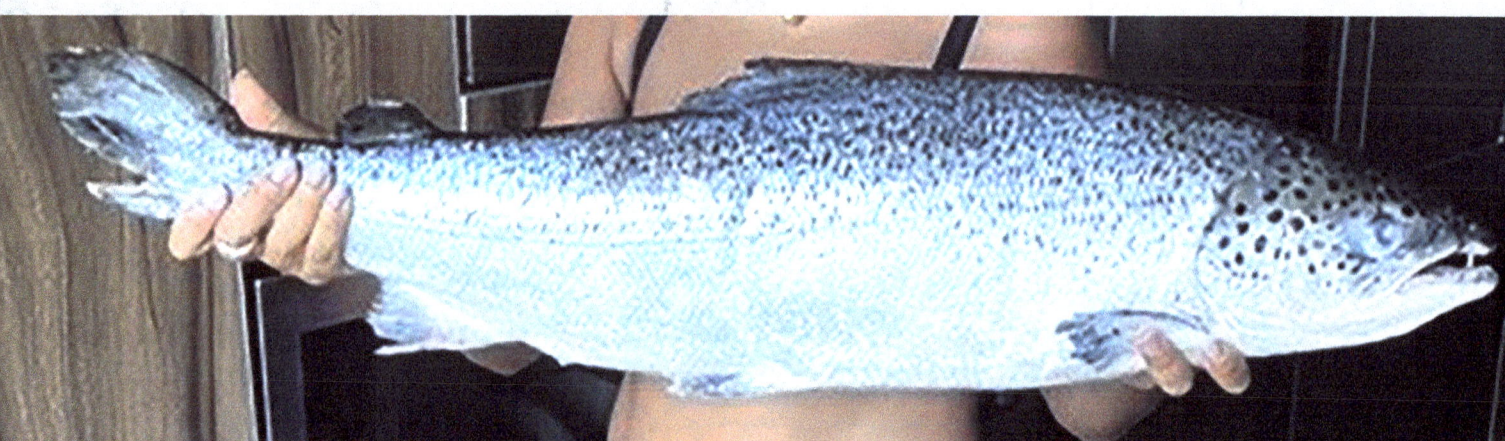

Chickpea Falafel

~~~~~~

1 **pound dry chickpeas**
1 ½ **cup parsley** *stems removed*
1 **cup cilantro** *stems removed*
1 **large onion**
8 **garlic cloves**
1 **tablespoon salt**
2 **teaspoons cumin seed or powder**
1 **tsp cardamon**
2 **teaspoons coriander**
1 **teaspoon black pepper**
1 **teaspoon baking powder**

1. **Soak dry chickpeas with enough water to cover them completely** at room temperature. After a few hours (ideally overnight), the chickpeas absorbe most of the water and doubles in size. Don't cook the chickpeas. They will stay raw, but soaking them will soften them enough to use in this recipe

2. Blend chickpeas to a grainy texture in food processor. (Not mush) Next, **add the herbs, onions, garlic, and seasoning.** It works well if you can blend on low or pulse at this point. You want the mixture to get blended but not overly soft and mushy. You're looking for a coarse paste

3. **Transfer to a bowl, cover and refrigerate then freeze the falafel mixture** in a freezer-safe bag or container. It will keep well for up to 3 months.

4. When you're ready to fry or bake the falafel, remove from the fridge, mix in some baking powder and form the patties or round circles.

5. You can also use an ice cream scooper, two spoons or your hands. While you're forming the patties, you can lay them on parchment paper or wax paper.

6. **Heat the oil slowly over medium heat for a couple minutes until it's hot. Then slowly fry the patties small batches at a time about 2-3 minutes per side.** The color will turn golden brown, then you'll know. Rest them on a paper towel to absorb the excess oil and then serve warm!

The difference between Chickpea Falafel recipe and a very Green falafel is that one is round & coated in breadcrumbs, and the other is the Mediterranean version Which would be in flatter Size, more authentic to the Mediterranean. The result is to directly Pan fry. Both can be frozen for storage Solutions and batch cooking.

A Very Green Falafel Recipe

A very green falafel recipe. We usually prefer our falafel in round balls rather than a flat patty. Also use some faves bean and dried chickpeas.

2 cups dry chickpeas (soaked, cooked with liquid)

½ teaspoon baking soda

1 medium onion, roughly chopped

1 cup chopped fresh parsley

Whole head of garlic

½ cup fava beans (dried, soaked and cooked)

1 ½ tablespoon flour or chickpea flour

1 ¾ teaspoon salt

2 teaspoon cumin seed or powder

1 teaspoon ground coriander seed (or I substitute with coriander leaves)

¼ teaspoon cayenne pepper

Pinch of ground cardamom

1 teaspoon baking powder(optional – makes the falafel more fluffy)

Vegetable oil for frying

1. Pour the chickpeas and fava beans into a large bowl and cover them by about 5 of cold water. Add ½ tsp of baking soda to the water and stir. Cover bowl and soak overnight in a cool, dark place or chill in the refrigerator. The chickpeas should soak at least 12 hours and up to 24 hours, until tender (change soaking water for fresh water also)

2. Drain and rinse the chickpeas and fava well. Pour them into your food processor along with the chopped onion, garlic cloves, parsley, flour or chickpea flour salt, cumin, coriander, black pepper, cayenne pepper, and cardamom

3. Process in a blender or food processor all ingredients together until a rough, coarse texture forms. Scrape the sides of the processor periodically and push the mixture down the sides. Process until the mixture is somewhere between the texture of couscous and a paste. You want the mixture to hold

4. Cover the bowl with plastic wrap and refrigerate for 1-2 hours already balled and rounded in the fridge.

5. Fill a skillet with oil to a depth of 1 ½ inches. Use cooking oil with a high smoke point (oil suggestions can be found in the ingredient list). Heat the oil slowly over medium heat. The ideal temperature to fry falafel is between 360 and 375 degrees. fry the falafels in batches of 5-6 at a time until golden brown on both sides. Once the falafels are fried, remove them from the oil using a slotted spoon. Let them drain & serve hot.

A Fluffy Hummus Recipe

½ pound dried chickpeas (soaked overnight and cooked) with some liquid of the soak

1 tablespoon baking soda

7 large garlic cloves, unpeeled

½ cup extra-virgin olive oil

¼ teaspoon ground cumin, plus more for garnish

½ cup tahini, at room temperature (see note)

¼ cup plus 1 tablespoon fresh lemon juice

Kosher salt

Paprika, for garnish

¼ cup chopped parsley

Soaking : Soak the dried chickpeas with 2 inches of water and stir in the baking soda. Refrigerate the chickpeas overnight. Drain the chickpeas and rinse them under cold water.

1. In a medium saucepan, cover the chickpeas with 2 inches of fresh water. Add the garlic cloves and bring to a boil. Simmer over moderately low heat until the chickpeas are tender, about 40 minutes. Drain, reserving 10 tablespoons of the cooking water and 2 tablespoons of the chickpeas. Rinse the chickpeas under cold water. Peel the garlic cloves.
2. In a food processor, purée the chickpeas with ½ cup of the reserved cooking water, ¼ cup of the olive oil and 6 of the garlic cloves. Add the cumin along with ¼ cup each of the tahini and lemon juice and process until creamy. Season the hummus with salt and transfer to a serving bowl.
3. Wipe out the food processor. Add the remaining ¼ cup of tahini, ¼ cup of olive oil, 2 tablespoons of reserved cooking water, 1 tablespoon of lemon juice and garlic clove and purée.
4. Using a ladle, make an indent in the center of the hummus. Spoon in the tahini-lemon mixture. Sprinkle the hummus with the cumin and paprika. Garnish with the reserved whole chickpeas and the parsley, and serve with pita or flatbread recipe

Beetroot Hummus Recipe

2 cups cooked chickpeas with some liquid

15 oz canned beets, drained (or 8 oz fully cooked and cooled beets)

½ cup tahini paste

1 small garlic clove

Juice of ½ lemon, more if needed

Kosher salt

½ tsp each cumin, coriander, and sumac (optional)

2 ice cubes or cold water

Extra virgin olive oil

1. In the large bowl of a food processor fitted with blade, place chickpeas, cooked beets, tahini, garlic, lemon juice. Season with salt and spices.
2. Run processor for a bit, and while it's running, add 2 ice cubes (this helps whip the beet hummus to a nice creamy consistency.)
3. Taste and adjust seasonings to your liking. Run processor again if the hummus is too thick yet, adding a little more ice as it runs (you can let it run for 4 minutes or so until you reach your desired creamy texture.)
4. Transfer beet hummus to a bowl. Drizzle extra virgin olive oil. Sprinkle feta and parsley on top. Serve with pita wedges or homemade pita chips and veggies for dipping.

The difference in the beetroot hummus is using tahini and the Mediterranean dip is a purely beetroot recipe.

Mediterranean Beetroot Hummus

6 small roasted beet

1 ½ cup cooked chickpeas

1 large lemon (zested)

½ large lemon (juiced)

1 healthy pinch salt and black pepper

5 large cloves garlic (minced)

¾ cup tahini

¼ cup extra virgin olive oil

1. Blend beetroot in a food processor until grainy. Add chickpeas next
2. Add remaining ingredients except for olive oil and blend until smooth.
3. Drizzle in olive oil as the hummus is mixing. Taste and adjust seasonings as needed, adding more salt, lemon juice, or olive oil if needed. If it's too thick, add a bit of water.

Flatbread Dough

1 teaspoon active dry or instant
    yeast
1 teaspoon granulated sugar
¾ cup (180ml) warm water,
    (between 100-110°F, 38-43°C)
2 cups (250g) all-purpose flour or
    bread flour, 00 works too. plus
    more for hands and surface
1 Tablespoon (15ml) olive oil, plus
    2 teaspoons for brushing the
    dough
1 teaspoon salt

1. Mix the dough ingredients together by hand or use a stand mixer. Can Knead by hand or beat the dough with your mixer.
2. Place dough into a greased mixing bowl, cover tightly, and let it rise for 45 minutes.
3. Punch down the slightly risen dough to release air bubbles. Divide in half. Let rise for another 10 min.
4. Flatten the two doughs with your hands or with a rolling pin. The flatbreads can be any shape you want as long as they're about ½ inch thick. Brush with olive oil, which helps protect the crust from any sogginess lingering from the toppings.
5. Shape accordingly - weather long or round pizza
6. Top with favorite toppings.
7. Bake at a very high temperature for only about 20 minutes or until lightly browned.

Prepare the dough: Whisk the yeast, sugar, and warm water together in the bowl of your stand mixer. Loosely cover and allow to sit for 5–10 minutes until foamy and frothy on top.

* If you do not own a stand mixer, you can do this in a large mixing bowl and in the next step, mix the dough together with spatula and hands. Add the flour, olive oil, and salt (and garlic/seasoning if using). Mix on low speed with the dough hook attachment until combined, about 2 minutes. The dough should be thick, yet soft and slightly sticky. It should pull away from the sides of the bowl as it mixes. When it does, it is ready to knead. If, however, the dough is too sticky to handle, mix in more flour, 1 Tablespoon at a time. Make sure you do not add too much extra flour; you want a soft dough

Knead the dough: Keep the dough in the mixer and beat with the dough hook on low speed for an additional 10 min or knead by hand on a lightly floured surface for 10 minutes. After kneading, the dough should still feel a little soft. Poke it with your finger—if it slowly bounces back, your dough is ready to rise.

You can also do a "windowpane test" to see if your dough has been kneaded long enough: tear off a small (roughly golfball-size) piece of dough and gently stretch it out until it's thin enough for light to pass through it. Hold it up to a window or light. Does light pass through the stretched dough without the dough tearing first? If so, your dough has been kneaded long enough and is ready to rise. If not, keep kneading.

Place the dough in a greased bowl (I use nonstick spray to grease) and cover with plastic wrap, aluminum foil, or a clean kitchen towel. Allow to sit and rest for 45 minutes at room temperature. Once it has rested and slightly risen, you can continue with the recipe or place the covered dough in the refrigerator for up to 2 days.

As the dough is resting and rising, prepare your toppings.

Preheat oven to 475°F (246°C).

Shape the dough: Punch the dough down to release any air. Divide the dough in half. On a lightly floured surface with floured hands and working with one dough piece at a time, begin shaping and stretching the dough until it is ¼ inch thick. You can use a floured rolling pin for this too. Don't worry about the shape of the dough, just make sure it's thin.

Shape/roll out the doughs directly on a baking mat or a large sheet of parchment then just transfer to baking sheet

Poke your fingers all around the surface of the flatbreads or . Drizzle or brush each with 1 teaspoon of olive oil. Top each with your favorite toppings.

If your shaping a longer elongated dough, give a thicker edge to the ends and oil. If your doing a round dough, we usually give a mound marker for the crusted edges and Let it sit and prove longer before putting inside high Heated oven at 400 degrees. The pizzas should cook in 4 minutes in a high heat oven.

Flatbread with Roasted Garlic, Sun-dried Tomato and Bufala Cheeses

1 large head garlic, unpeeled

2 tbsps.olive oil

1 large red onion, cut into ½-inch-thick rings

50 grams of sun-dried tomato, drained, oil reserved

125 grams bufala mozzarella cheese

50 grams pine-nuts

10 leaf of fresh basil

2 tbsps. chopped fresh oregano

1. Preheat oven to 195°C. Slice top off garlic head; place in small baking dish. Drizzle with 1 tablespoon olive oil. Brush baking sheet with ½ tablespoon olive oil. Place onion slices on sheet and brush onion with ½ tablespoon olive oil. Bake garlic and onion until garlic cloves are light brown and soft and onion is tender, about 45 minutes. Remove from oven; let cool.

2. Using fingers, squeeze out roasted garlic cloves into food processor; add sun-dried tomatoes. Using on/off turns, process until almost smooth, adding enough reserved oil form sun-dried tomatoes to form paste.

3. Preheat oven to 220°C. Place crust on baking sheet or pizza pan. Spread garlic paste evenly over crust. Top with slice of Bufala mozzarella cheese, roasted pine-nuts. Sprinkle with 10 basil leaf and 1 tablespoon fresh oregano.

4. Bake the flatbread until crust is golden brown and cheese bubbles, about 5 minutes. Transfer to cutting board. Cool 5 minutes. Sprinkle with remaining 2 tablespoons basil and 1 tablespoon fresh Oregano.

Anzani Cheese Fundue

½ cup raclette cheese grated

½ cup emmental cheese grated

½ cup Gruyère cheese grated

½ cup white wine or kirsch

diced shallot /or white onion

1 bay leaf

Dash of cream

1. Sauté onion, bay leaf, add white wine (Krish) reduce over low flame, add cheese
2. Mix throughly until it resembles a sauce like reduction. If the cheeses are too thick add a dash of cream
3. Transfer to fondue pot with heat element keep stirring
4. Serve with square crusty bread

An serve with boiled vegetables or potatoes

44

Tuscan Bean Soup

This soup is made with borlotti beans, If you cant find them. You can choose to use White canneli beans or pinto beans. We usually prefer dried beans soaked overnight. But If unable grocery stores sell them canned. Make sure to rinse wash and soak in clear water before using.

1 large White onion
5 garlic cloves minced
2.5 cups borlotti beans dried (and
   If canned-2.5 cups also)
2 Tbsp fennel seeds (toasted)
¼ cup bacon (½inch thick
7-8 Tbsp tomato paste double
   concentrated
1 Tbsp flaked chili
2-3 strips lemon peel
3 sprigs fresh rosemary
2 bay leaves
3 tsp onion powder
7-8 cups water
½ bunch Italian parsley roughly
   chopped
S + P to taste
2.5 cups borlotti beans

Rinse and soak the borlotti beans in cold water for 6 hours or overnight. Drain and rinse again.

1. Preheat a heavy bottom soup pot over medium heat with a drizzle of olive oil and saute the onion or leek until softened and begins to get some color around the edges.
2. Stir in the fennel seeds and toast around until fragrant then add the garlic. Cook another minute or so until you can smell the garlic. 5 garlic cloves, 2 Tbsp fennel seeds. In another Pan saute the bacon into strips you want the flavour from the Meat to create another dimension
3. Add the tomato paste (+ chili paste if using) and toss to coat well with the onion mixture. 7-8 Tbsp tomato paste, 1 Tbsp chili
4. Add the soaked beans to the pot together with the rosemary, bay leaves, lemon peel and onion powder. Pour in the water and bring to a boil. Cover with a lid and keep at a a constant boil for 45 minutes stirring now and then. 2.5 cups borlotti beans, 2-3 strips lemon peel, 3 sprigs fresh rosemary, 2 bay leaves, 3 tsp onion powder, 7-8 cups water
5. Check the beans in 45 minute and season with a pinch of good sea salt. Continue cooking an addition 15 to 30 minutes or until the beans are buttery soft to your liking. S + P to taste. Save some onion, cooked beans for the side for those that like soups with texture.
6. Blend in food processor. Remove from heat, adjust seasonings with salt and pepper and stir in the parsley. Serve with side compliment of cooked beans on a Plate

Pork Tomahawk with Chiken Mushroom

Ask your butcher to give you a 1 ½ inch pork cutlet and French the bone.

1 kilo French pork rack cutlet cut at 1 ½ inch thickness.
Salt /pepper
Butter
Breadcrumbs
2 eggs

1. Season with salt and pepper
2. Marinate and do an egg wash, first bathe in egg wash, then roll in
3. Roll in breadcrumbs.
4. Add butter and oil to a pan and pan fry until golden brown
5. In a heated oven (175 degrees) place plan or tray in oven and cook further for 15 minutes.
6. Sauté chicken mushrooms and score and plate with chicken mushrooms and serve the pork tomahawk standing with bone facing up

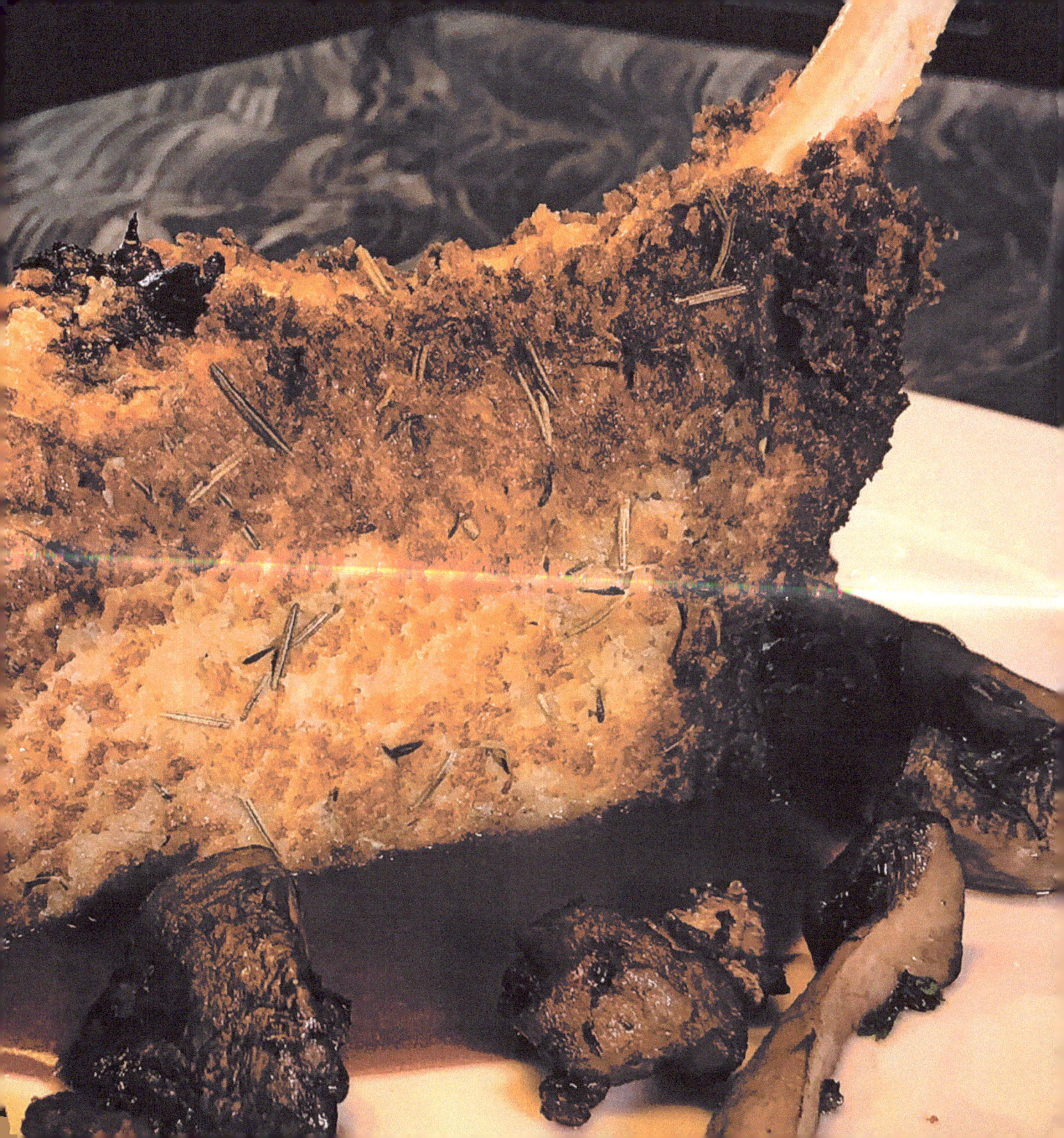

Angus Tenderloin with Cauliflower Steak and Harissa

1.5 kilo of Angus tenderloin
String

FOR CAULIFLOWER:
Cauliflower cut legnthwise in 1.5 inches thick
Olive oil
Lemon
Chopped parsley
Diced garlic

FOR HARISSA:
18 dried chiles de árbol
(Rehydrated)
1 can red peppers in can
2 dried ancho chiles
2 tbsp dried chilli seeds
2 tablespoon cumin seeds
1 tbsp coriander seeds
5 garlic cloves, smashed
2 tablespoons fresh lemon juice
1 tablespoon white wine vinegar
1 tablespoon tomato paste
2 teaspoons hot smoked Spanish paprika
1 teaspoon kosher salt
¾ cup olive oil, divided

1. Marinated in salt pepper and white pepper. Marinate. String the tenderloin so all areas of the tenderloin are even sized rounds
2. Tie legnthwise then, sections of horizontal sections to hold its shape.
3. Sear over high heat with olive oil and butter. After seared brown. Slice the rounds 2 inches thick. The tenderloin will be cooked medium rare. If it needs more cooking seal both ends until brown

CAULIFLOWER MARINATION:
1. Marinate overnight.
2. Sear and grill cauliflower steaks and cook to tender.

HARISSA RECIPE :
1. Place all dried chiles in a large glass. Pour ½ cup boiling water over to rehydrate, let sit until chiles are "coming back to life " enough to handle. Drain;
2. Toast cumin and coriander in a dry small skillet over medium-low heat, until toasted. Transfer to a food processor, add garlic, and blend until spices are broken up and garlic forms a paste. Add chiles and pulse until chiles form a coarse paste. Add lemon juice, vinegar, tomato paste, paprika, and salt and process until mostly smooth but mixture still has a little texture. stream in ½ cup oil. Taste. It should have a mild spicy flavour but not overpowering

Pork Belly Roast with Purple Yam and Banana Blossom

1 kilo pork belly whole
Brining liquid
Bay leaves
Salt / sugar (1 tbsp each)

FOR PURPLE YAM:
1 kilo boiled purple yam
1 cup milk
3 tbsp grated garlic
Bay leaf
Banana blossom dehydrated

1. Boil the pork belly under tender and fat is soft.
2. Score the top of the skin to long cuts that it resembles lines
3. Heat oven to 180 degrees and crisp the skin and fully crispy. In the oven. We usually use the gratinator to guarantee skin bubbles and nice long lines in its cooking for presentation

PURPLE YAM:
1. Add Milk, garlic, bay leaf and dehydrated banana blossom in simmer. Salt.
2. Chop the yam. Take out the bay leaf and banana blossom and blend to mashed levels of consistency.
3. There will be a purple mash with scents of caramelized with a herby and garlic infusion. It's simply unique. The colour pops
4. Serve crispy pork belly over the purple mash. Drizzle with caramelized balsalmic glaze (balsamic vinegar, 1 tbsp of palm sugar, drizzle olive oil)

Steak on Grill with Herb Butter and Rosemary

~~~~~~

It's really important to make sure your steaks are at room temperature before cooking them. Remove them from the fridge and let them sit at room temperature for up to an hour before cooking

Tenderloin Steaks

FOR HERBED BUTTER:
Fresh Tarragon
Handful of parsley
Handful of rosemary
Lemon rind
Salt
Block of butter

HERBED BUTTER:
1. Blend in processor. Scoop in plastic glad wrap and create a long cylinder and roll both ends and twist both ends to create a tight cylinder (should be the shape of a tube)
2. Refrigerate.

STEAK:
1. Pat steaks dry. Season steaks with onion powder, garlic powder, salt and black pepper with a dash of smoked paprika
2. Fire up grill to high temperature at 400 degrees so that when you drop the steaks you achieve grill marks.
3. Depending on your cut and thickness and desired doneness. We like our steaks medium rare.
4. If your cut is ½ inch thick or 1 inch in thickness. You will need to grill in 2 minutes to get grill marks. It's important to let your steaks rest to absorb all juices and keep in flavour
5. Add herbed butter when serving.

Guaranteed. Extra fine levels and dimensions in eating steak.

Chicken Tangine with Preserved Lemons

1 kilo quarter cut chicken leg,
1 tbsp vegetable oil
1 onion, sliced
2 garlic cloves, crushed
1 tsp ground cinnamon
1 tsp ground cumin
1 tsp ground ginger
1 tsp ground turmeric
1 tsp chilli flakes
450ml/16fl oz chicken stock
6 halves dried preserved lemons

*can make your own preserved
lemon by cutting in half 3 lemons
and slow simmer in ½ cup salt and
adding ½ cup water - will achieve
a salty syrup consistency - can be
done in advance and put in jars)
the longer you have in your kitchen
the better)

salt and freshly ground black
    pepper
2 tbsp freshly chopped mint
2 tbsp freshly chopped parsley

1. Marinate chicken in the spices overnight & refrigerate.
2. Sear the chicken in high heat.
3. Add chicken stock, add preserved lemons, add chickpeas
4. Cook in Tangine pot on low heat for 1 hour. It will be the most delicious melt in your mouth creation. The stock will reduce to a unique blend with Lemon halves and not dry.

Lamb Tangine with Prunes

4 lamb legs
6 garlic cloves, chopped
2 tbsp (30 ml) olive oil
1 tbsp sweet paprika
1 tbsp ground ginger
2 tsp ground cinnamon
2 tsp ground turmeric
2 cups (500 ml) chicken broth/beef broth
1 cup (200 g) pitted prunes
¼ cup (40 g) roasted blanched almonds
2 tbsp (30 ml) honey

1. Sear the lamb in salt and pepper and brown.
2. In the same Tangine base, sauté garlic, olive oil, paprika, ginger, cinnamon, tumeric and bring to boil. Then simmer the lamb with prunes. And almonds and honey
3. Leave in Tangine pot for an hour.
4. Serve with couscous or a bed of parsley pilaf rice.

We had to soak the Tangine pots in a bathtub to be able to do batch cooking and be able to ensure that the the pots hold well in double or triple use cooking to cook batches of Tangine

Beef Kabob Morrocan Spices

2 kilo ground beef (or ground
   lamb)
fresh garlic cloves
onions
fresh parsley
fresh mint
fresh cilantro
sweet paprika (or smoked paprika)
cumin powder
Cumin seed
Fresh turmeric
salt
black pepper
red pepper flakes. (if you like heat,
   you can add a little cayenne
Dried Roses
Cardamon seeds

1. Marinate the meat in all the toasted spices that have been through a heated pan to bring out flavour. Keep in fridge overnight.
2. Flatten the beef in a skewer or stick. Put in a grill setting in the oven.
3. Serve with tahini yoghurt and chopped mint.

Pumpkin Flowers Stuffed with Ricotta Cheese

Friturra Fiori di zucchini (pumpkin flowers)

This delicate dish is so intense and unimaginable that the Italians have mastered a method of cooking that captures essence and finesse.

8 zucchini flowers
1 tub ricotta cheese
Flaky Salt
Grated Parmesan cheese
Grated lemon skills of 1 whole lemon
Chopped parsley

FOR THE FRITTER :
90 gms plain flour, refrigerated
140 mls sparkling water, refrigerated
flaked sea salt

1. Stuff the ricotta paste or pipe into the zucchini flower
2. Dip the stuffed zucchini flower in the flour paste, and quick fry in oil. It should crisp but not brown

Serve immediately.

Lobster Risotto with Adlai in Saffron Sauce

Lobster broth
Water
4-5 Lobster Tails (approximately
 1 ¼ pounds with shells on) or 1
 whole lobster like picture above.
 It weighed 1.7 kg
2 cups Adlai that have been soaked
 overnight
Kosher Salt
1/2 cup Dry White Wine
Shallots or Yellow Onion, finely
 diced
Unsalted Butter
Canola Oil
1 tbsp of Saffron threads
Parmesan Cheese, grated
Garnish: diced Italian parsley

1. In a stock pot with 4 cups water over medium-low heat; bring to a gentle simmer. Add lobster Shell and Head after a good clean of the lobster Head. Simmer until you get a good broth
2. Preparing the Shell: Get a sharp, heavy knife split the lobster tail shells lengthwise. Take out the lobster Meat and separate.
3. Using your hands, remove the meat from the shell (does not. *Reserve tail shells.*
4. If the lobster has a large vein (which is really the lobster's intestine) on the back of the meat remove it and discard
5. Cut lobster meat into bite sized pieces. Place in a bowl, cover and refrigerate until needed.
6. You Will need the Shell and Head of lobster to make the lobster broth. Simmer until you have achieved lobster stock
7. In a large saute Pan or Casserole over medium high heat, combine 3 tablespoons butter and 3 tablespoons canola oil, stirring until butter melts.
8. In a separate small mixing bowl, rub a large pinch of saffron threads between thumb and forefinger to break up the threads; add to bowl. Add ½ cup of the simmering stock to crushed saffron.
9. To the large saute Pan add diced shallots or onion. Sauté, stirring frequently until translucent (about 2-3 minutes); do not brown.
10. Add adlai to saute oven. Stir to coat fully with butter-oil-shallot mixture. Stir over medium-high heat for 2-3 minutes.
11. Pour white wine into Dutch oven, cooking stirring constantly until liquid evaporates
12. Add ¼ cup stock to adlai mixture, stirring until absorbed. Repeat, continuing to add stock and stir until liquid is absorbed.

13. Pour in crushed saffron and stock mixture. Stir until liquid is absorbed.

14. After 18 minutes Continue to add stock, stirring until liquid is absorbed.

15. Taste the adlai around 20 minutes and when it is 'al dente', soft but still with structure in the middle, the lobster should be added. ***If it is not yet this texture*** at 20 minutes, continue to add stock, letting it absorb, tasting the rice until the desired texture is reached to add the lobster. *If you run out of stock before the rice reaches the desired consistency, add water ¼ cup at a time until the Adlai is 'al dente'.*

16. Cook the Adlai with the lobster added, stirring constantly for 5 minutes.

17. After 5 minutes, turn off the heat and stir in the parmesan cheese, 1 tablespoon of butter, salt and pepper to taste. Serve in Its Shell. Serves 8 people

Smoked Ribs

2 kilo ribs (not split in half)

FOR THE SAUCE:
1 cup soy
½ cup ketchup
½ cup grainy mustard
1 tbsp red vinegar

1. Marinate ribs in smoke liquid with salt and pepper overnight
2. Cook the ribs over high heat grill. Then finish in the oven with sauce in 30 minutes.
3. Serve as the meat falls off the bone. So simple, but the technique with the smoking liquid adds a different dimension.

Serve to a big family.

Crispy Roll of Pork with Figs, Prunes and Almonds stuffed with Herbed Lemon Bread Stuffing

1 pork belly, skin on (800 - 1.2kg / 1.6 - 2.4 lb)
1 ½ tbsp balsalmic vinegar
1 tsp black pepper
1 tsp white pepper
½ tsp salt

FOR SALT COVER:
200 g / 7 oz rock salt

FOR THE STUFFING:
2 cups breadcrumbs
½ stick butter
Rosemary /
Sage/thyme
3 tbsp grated lemon
½ cup apricot (soaked)
½ cup fig (soaked)
½ cup prunes
½ cup whole almonds (toasted)

COOK:
1. Preheat oven to 180C/350F (all oven types).
2. Remove pork from fridge. Place onto a large sheet of foil. Fold up sides of foil around the pork tor the salt bake. Cover with salt completely
3. Transfer pork to baking tray. Dab skin with paper towels.
4. Brush skin with vinegar.
5. Spread rock salt on the skin (the foil edges will stop it from falling down the sides).
6. Roast for 60 minutes.
7. Remove pork from oven and transfer onto work surface.
8. Switch to grill/broiler on medium high. Move shelf so it is at least 25cm/10" from the heat source.
9. Fold down foil and scrape all the salt off the top and sides. Return pork only (already rolled) to baking tray.
10. Place under grill or top head for 20 - 25 minutes in oven rotating tray once, until skin is golden, crispy and puffed.

STUFFING:
1. 2 cups Breadcrumbs ½ stick of butter Rosemary/ sage/thyme 3 tbsp Grated lemon rind ½ cup Apricot ½ cup dried figs ½ cup whole almonds ½ cup prunes Salt
2. Blend all ingredients in a food processor. You will achieve a paste. Use this paste when rolling pork belly stuffing. Chop apricots, figs and prunes to add texture and some chopped almonds on top of the paste when rolling

The trick is to Prick a lot of holes in the skin to get the puffy crackling with bubbles. (You can use a pick or sharp edge of a fondue stick or bbq stick. Roast first covered in rock salt first to achieve crispy crackling. The pork belly is first roasted with the salt crust, then the salt crust is removed. the skin will look rubbery. Roll the belly to a cylinder and put the stuffing in the roll. Tie so the roll so it will hold its shape. You will want to achieve a rolled cylindrical shape that has been tied by string to hold its shape. Place under the grill/broiler for 25 minutes until the cackling comes out even in colour and crispness is achieved.

Black Cod wrapped in Potato Spaghetti with Lemon and White Wine Reduction

~~~~~~~~~~~~~~~~~~~~~~~~~~~~~~~

150 grams Chilean sea bass

1 piece ripe roma tomato

20 milliliter olive oil

2 teaspoons basil leaves

2 teaspoons lemon zest

3 teaspoons finely chopped garlic

1 teaspoon finely chopped thyme herb

½ liter vegetable oil (for Frying)

2 teaspoons finely chopped parsley 1 pinch sea salt

¼ teaspoon white pepper

50 grams sweet potato

25 grams Spanish chorizo

20 grams wild arugula leaves

5 grams butter

2 pieces lemon

1. Sauté onion, bay leaf, add white wine (Krish) reduce over low flame, add cheese
2. Mix throughly until it resembles a sauce like reduction. If the cheeses are too thick add a dash of cream
3. Transfer to fondue pot with heat element keep stirring
4. Serve with square crusty bread

An serve with boiled vegetables or potatoes

Cauliflower Veloute and Kale Bed with Smoked Lobster Meat and Edible Flowers

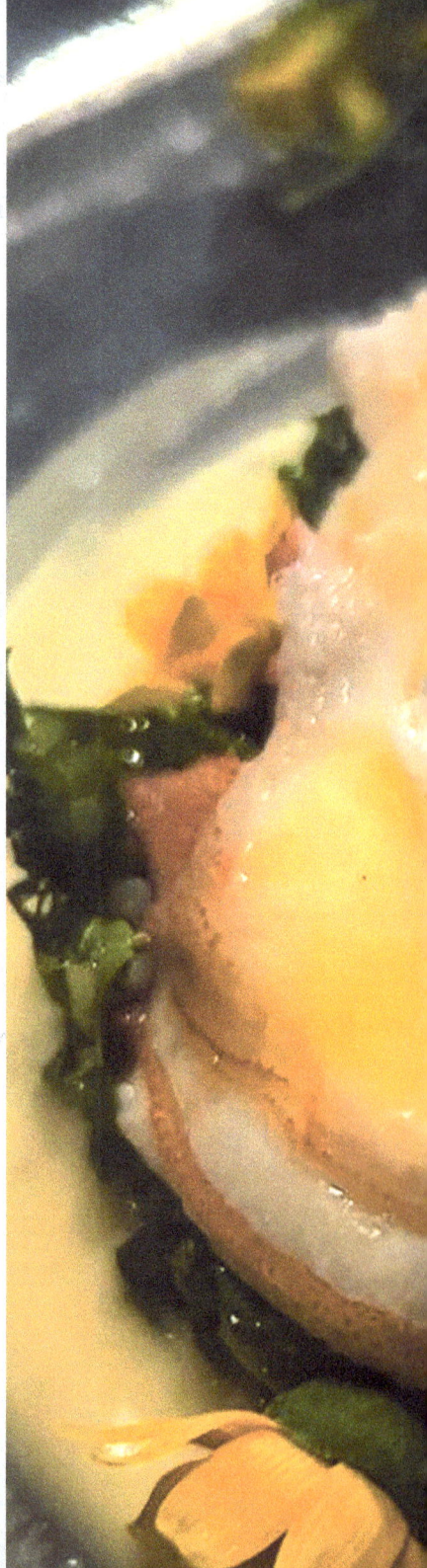

500g cauliflower florets, roughly chopped
40 grams Butter
75 grams Mascarpone cheese
salt and pepper to taste

1. Braise the cauliflower with butter till fully cooked. Blended with mascarpone add seasoning.

2. Smoke the lobster tails. Preheat it and keep it at 120°C. This low temperature is harder to maintain, but we want to allow the lobster time to absorb the flavor without cooking it too quickly, approximately 60 minutes of cook time.

3. Place the lobster tails directly on the grill grate in the smoker and close.

4. Finished by quick sautéed bites size lobster medallion on Lemon butter sauce, plated on the cauliflower veloute decorated with edible flowers

Beetroot Caramele Pasta

500 grams ripe beetroot roasted in oven peeled and puréed
6 eggs (whole)
500 grams semolina flour
750 00 flour
2 tsp evo
2 pinch of salt

FOR THE STUFFING:
500 grams fresh ricotta
Sauté with chopped white onion
Fresh dill
Sauce / lemon sauce
Lemon zest
Lemon juice
Butter
Parmesan cheese

1. Mix ingredients for pasta dough
2. Let the dough rest for 1-2 hours
3. Open in very thin sheet
4. Cut out rectangular shape (6 cm by 4 cm) brush with egg wash
5. Pipe 4cm long ricotta mix with dill salt & pepper
6. Roll over pasta dough and twist like candy wrapper
7. Boil for 5 min in salt water
8. Strain then place in sauté pan with pre melted butter with lemon zest
9. Add Carmelle sprinkle with Parmesan cheese (grated) serve

Ravioli

FOR THE PASTA DOUGH:
Cups all-purpose flour
2 cups 00 Flour
2 large eggs
1 Tbsp cold water
Pinch of salt

FOR THE FILLING:
½ cup ricotta cheese
5.5 oz fresh spinach (squeeze all water out)
½ cup Parmigiano Reggiano cheese
½ tsp ground nutmeg
Salt and pepper

1. Sprinkle some flour on a working surface. Divide the dough into 3 parts so it is more manageable. Leave two portions well covered with cling film to prevent them from drying out.

2. Roll the dough into two long rectangular sheets about 1mm thick (a little less than 1/16-inch). You can use a pasta machine or do it by hand with a rolling pin.

3. On one of the sheets, place small mounds using a mini ice cream a Cooper of the ricotta and spinach filling, leaving about 3cm (1.2-inch) of empty space between them.

4. Moist the dough between each portion and around the filling with a bit of water, you can use a brush or your fingers.

5. The Size of the sheet should be able to make opposite ends meet and seal one end with water and take the other end. It should be a pointed rise. Example 1,4 ends should meet 2,3 should meet. (If the square is 1.2,3,4 ends)

6. Now, place ravioli on a plate or tray floured with a little semolina or all-purpose flour to prevent them from sticking together. Must always rest the ravioli for an hour. Before cooking

Basic Pasta Dough Recipe

400 g Italian soft wheat flour '00'(14oz) All purpose flour can be used too.
4 eggs large
1 pinch salt

1. To make the pasta, mound your flour on a large wooden board. Make a well in the center and add a pinch of salt.
2. Break the eggs into the well and whisk them a little (you can also beat eggs in a small bowl and then add to flour or start by mixing flour and eggs together in a bowl and then turn out onto a board to knead)
3. Start to incorporate the eggs and flour by slowly bringing more flour in from the inside edges of the well. You can use a fork or scraper for this.
4. Continue mixing the flour with the eggs until they are no longer runny.
5. Using your hands now, bring the outside edges in, forming a large mass on your board.
6. Begin to knead the dough as you would bread, pushing it down with the heel of your hand.
7. Continue kneading for about 7-10 minutes. Knead until the pasta dough is smooth, elastic, and just slightly tacky. You can dust the dough with more flour if it's too sticky, but try not to add too much additional flour or the pasta will be tough.
8. Roll the dough into a ball and wrap it in cling film and let it sit for about 30 minutes.
9. Cut off 1/6 of the dough, re-wrap the rest in cling film so it doesn't dry out and roll out the piece you cut off until it is flat enough that you can pass it through a pasta machine if you are using one.
10. I used my pasta machine to roll out the sheets, first 3-4 times on number 6 or 7 on the dial (widest setting) and then a couple of times more on number 4. Each time you pass the dough through the machine fold it first into thirds and pass it through again until it comes out with the right thickness and length. If you want even thinner sheets you can also pass the dough through again on number 2 or 3. Cut the sheet to the length you want.
11. If you aren't using a machine you need to keep rolling out the dough until it is thin enough to almost see your fingers through it. Then cut the sheet to the size you want.
12. Transfer the ready sheets to a drying rack while you prepare the rest. Repeat with the remaining dough

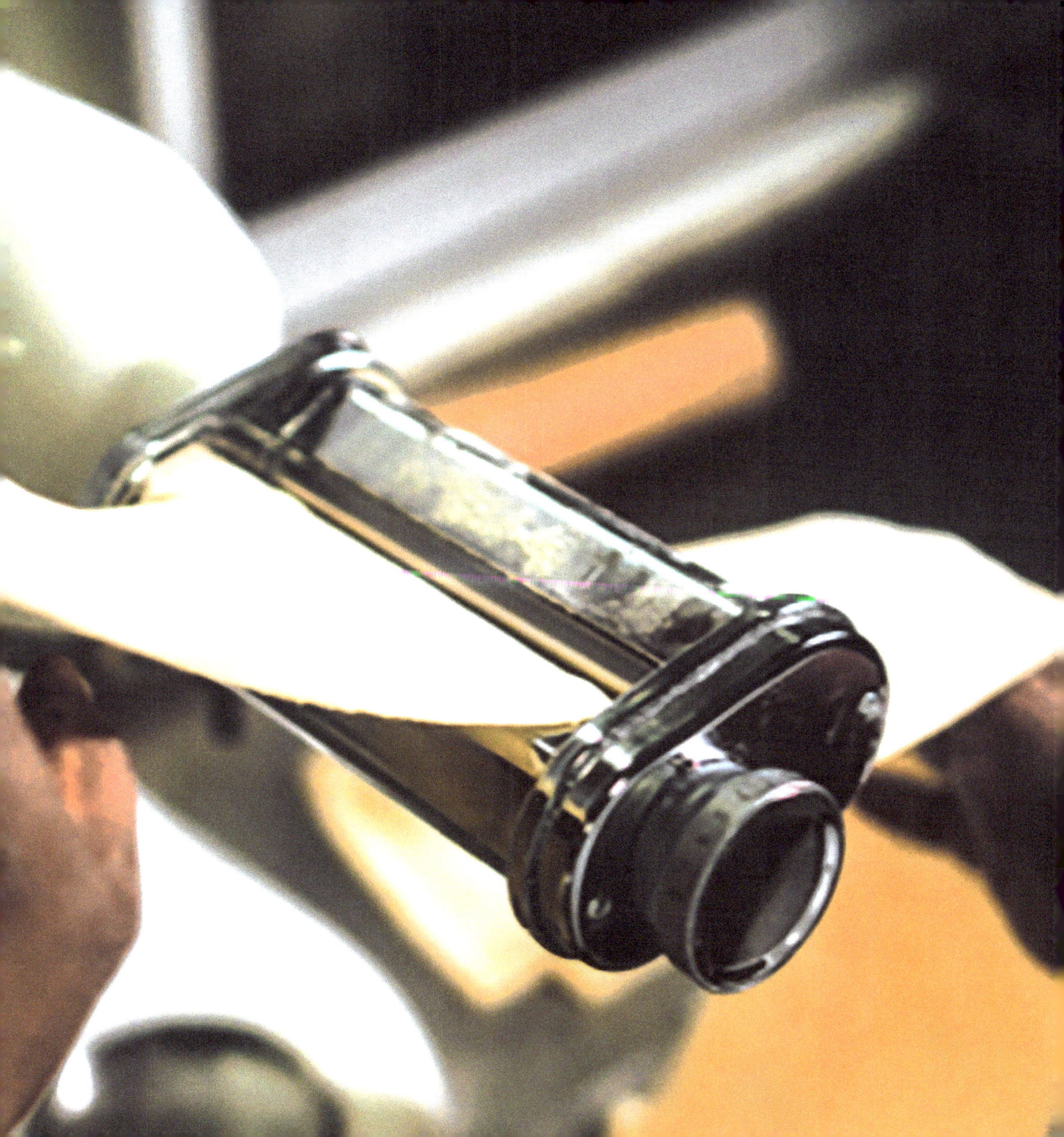

Egg Pasta Dough

300 grams "00" flour
100 grams Semolina
    flour
5 grams sea salt
2 whole large eggs
8 egg yolks
2 tablespoon extra-virgin
    olive oil

1. Incorporate all ingredients until it resembles dough.
2. Use dough hook and process for 2 min
3. Using a pasta maker sheet. Run the dough through the machine until it thins.
4. Slice sheet into ½ inch cuts

Linguini Vogole

FOR THE EGG PASTA DOUGH:
300 grams "00" flour
100 grams Semolina flour
5 grams sea salt
2 whole large eggs
8 egg yolks
2 tablespoon extra-virgin olive oil

3 to 4 pounds littleneck clams,
   cleaned
1 pound fresh linguine
¼ cup olive oil, plus additional for
   serving
¼ cup butter
10 cloves garlic
¼ cup Diced White onion
¼ to ½ teaspoon crushed red
   pepper flakes (more or less, to
   taste)
1 ½ cup dry Sauvignon Blanc or
   Pino Grigio
¼ cup fresh lemon juice
3 tablespoons unsalted butter
⅓ cup chopped fresh parsley, plus
   2 tablespoons for garnish
kosher salt

EGG PASTA DOUGH
1. Incorporate all ingredients until it resembles dough.
2. Use dough hook and process for 2 min
3. Using a pasta maker sheet. Run the dough through the machine until it thins.
4. Slice sheet into ½ inch cuts

Use fresh Littleneck or Manila clams to make Linguine with Clams. Both of these varieties are delicate, sweet, andmeaty enough to not encourage chewy textures. Before cooking, it's important to clean live clams thoroughly so that sand doesn't find its way into your pasta. use a wide bottomed pan, like a 12-inch skillet. As a saute Pan.

1. While the pasta is cooking, in another pot. It Will take 4 Minutes to cook fresh PASTA. Strain and Drain. heat ¼ cup of olive oil in a deep skillet, sauté pan (12-14 inches wide). Add Onion, garlic and red pepper flakes and cook, stirring, until garlic is lightly-browned and fragrant, about 1-2 minutes. Add white wine, lemon juice, and clams, cover pan, and steam over medium-high heat until clamshells have opened, about 5-8 minutes.
2. The juices of the Pan pour into the cooked fresh PASTA.
3. Serve hot and the clams separate
4. The fresh PASTA Will absorb the juices. And immediately the PASTA Will take on a flavour. While the clams can get picked separately

Squid Ink Spaghetti

FOR THE BASE EGG YOLK PASTA:

10 ounces (about 2 cups) all-purpose flour, plus more for dusting

2 whole large eggs (about 4 ounces)

4 yolks from 4 large eggs (about 2.5 ounces)

ADD THE SQUID INK FOR "BLACK PASTA":

4 teaspoons squid ink

1 teaspoon kosher salt, plus more for salting water

To Make the Dough: On a large, clean work surface, pour flour in a mound. Make a well in the center about 4 inches wide. Pour whole eggs, egg yolks, squid ink, and salt into well and, using a fork, beat thoroughly. When combined, gradually incorporate flour into the eggs until a wet, sticky dough has formed.

1. Using a bench knife, scrape excess dough from fork and fingers. Begin to fold additional flour into the dough with the bench knife, turning the dough roughly 45 degrees each time, until dough feels firm and dry, and can form a ball, 2 to 5 minutes.

2. Press the heel of the hand into the ball of dough, pushing forward and down. Rotate the ball 45 degrees and repeat. Continue until dough develops a smooth, elastic texture. If dough feels too wet, add flour in 1 teaspoon at a time. If dough feels too dry, add water slowly using a spray bottle.

3. Wrap ball of dough tightly in plastic wrap and rest on countertop for 30 minutes. To Roll the Pasta: place a sheet of parchment paper on a tray or cutting board and dust lightly with flour. Unwrap rested dough and cut into quarters. Set one quarter on work surface and re-wrap remaining dough. With a rolling pin, flatten the quarter of dough into an oblong shape about ½ inch thick.

4. Set pasta maker to widest setting and pass dough 3 times through the machine at this setting.

5. Place dough on a lightly floured work surface. Fold both ends in so that they meet at the center of the dough, and then fold the dough in half where the end points meet, trying not to incorporate too much air into the folds. Using rolling pin, flatten dough to ½-inch thick. Pass through the rollers 3 additional times.

6. Narrow the setting by 1 notch and repeat Repeat once more (the dough should now have passed through the third widest setting). Continue

passing the dough through the rollers, reducing the thickness by 1 setting each time until it reaches the desired thickness. It should now be very delicate and elastic to the touch, and slightly translucent.

7. Place rolled dough onto a work surface or baking sheet lightly dusted with flour or lined with parchment paper, folding the dough over as necessary so that it fits; sprinkle with flour or line with parchment between folds to prevent sticking.

8. Cover dough with plastic wrap or a kitchen towel to prevent drying, then repeat Steps 5 through 9 with remaining dough quarters. If making noodles, cut dough into 12- to 14-inch segments.

9. To Cut Noodles: Adjust pasta machine to noodle setting of your choice. Working one dough segment at a time, feed dough through the pasta-cutter. Alternatively, cut folded dough by hand with a knife to desired noodle width

10. Divide the cut noodles into individual portions, dust lightly with flour, and curl into a nest. Place on parchment-lined rimmed baking sheet and gently cover with kitchen towel until ready to cook.

11. Pasta can be frozen directly on the baking sheet, transferred to a zipper-lock freezer bag, and stored in the freezer for up to three weeks before cooking.

12. Cook frozen pasta directly from the freezer.

Open Spinach Lasagna with Foie Gras and Truffle Cream

2 tablespoons olive oil

6 large onions, halved and thinly sliced

6 cloves garlic, chopped.

1 ½ cups chicken or vegetable stock, divided

6 scallions, thinly sliced

1 tablespoon dried oregano

2 teaspoons salt, plus more to season

1 teaspoon freshly ground black pepper, plus more to season

9 spinach homemade lasagna pasta cut in disk shape

200 grams fresh spinach

1 tablespoon salted butter

1 tablespoon all-purpose flour

1 egg

250 grams camembert cheese cut in cubes

250 grams row goose liver

Grated zest of ½ lemon

Olive oil cooking spray

1 cup grated Parmesan, divided

Heat oven to 175°C. In a large sauté pan over medium heat, heat oil. Add onions and garlic; toss to coat. Add 1 cup stock. Cover and reduce heat; simmer until onions are soft. 20 minutes. Reserve ½ cup liquid. Add scallions, oregano, salt, and pepper to onion mixture; increase heat to medium and cook, stirring, until liquid evaporates, 20 minutes. Cook lasagna disk pasta on salty boiling water for 3 minutes; drain and blot dry. Cook spinach on sauté: drain, squeeze dry and season with salt and pepper. Sear the goose liver precut in cube in very hot sauté wit little seasoning. In a small saucepan over medium heat, melt butter. Add flour; stir until rou is brown, 2 to 3 minutes. Add remaining ½ cup stock to reserved liquid; whisk into roux ur thick, 5 minutes. In a bowl, beat egg: stir in camembert cheese and the goose liver and zest. an oven tray pan with cooking spray, spread half of stock-roux mixture on bottom. Line up w 4 lasagna disk; layer on half of onion goose liver and camembert mixtures, half of spinach, c ⅓ cup Parmesan. Repeat layer with disk of spinach lasagna on each one, remaining onion. camembert mixtures and spinach, and ⅓ cup Parmesan. Top with remaining lasagna to noodles, half of stock-roux mixture, and ⅓ cup grated Parmesan. Bake until light brown minutes. Reduce heat to 150°C. Let lasagna sit 1 minute; serve garnished with sweet rod cherry tomato with thyme and truffle paste cream sauce.

Closing

The pandemic has taught us many things. We should all be eating better – healthier. It also reminded us why we do what we do. We still believe in rainbows, unicorn dreams, paradise beaches, marshmallow fluff.

Quarantine did not kill the spirit, just because dreams are just on hold for now. Essentially, food makes everyone happy.

In our home kitchen turned food lab, Marco and I experimented with curing (Salmon & Tanguige), smoking (beef ribs & pork shoulder) dehydrating (skin and root chips) fermenting (rice & vegetables) smoking meat, making cold press (juice had fun with "Apothecary" using plant as medicine extracts And Jus (Achuete extract/ turmeric oil/ pili nut & Acapulco infusion/ moringa powder/ mushroom broth).

Farmers who needed help bought from, and we birthed grocery gourmet meals called "Kain Na" and "Gusto" now found in groceries locally in Cebu and Manila.

Food needs to be fantasy, art, romance,
color, play, and fairy floss so that we
all remember – Dream First!

Then the universe answers you by doing the work.